Strange Science:
OUTER SPACE

▼

Q.L. PEARCE

Illustrated by Bernice Mascher

Reviewed and endorsed by
Alan Harris
Department of Earth and Planetary Physics Group,
Jet Propulsion Laboratory, Pasadena, California

TOR®

A TOM DOHERTY ASSOCIATES BOOK
NEW YORK

*To the students of Robert Clow Elementary
School, Napierville, Illinois, with thanks.*

—Q.L.P.

*To my parents, Hellmut and Elsie Mascher, who
initiated my first interest in space.*

—B.M.

STRANGE SCIENCE: OUTER SPACE

Copyright © 1999 by RGA Publishing Group, Inc.

Cover and interior art by Bernice Mascher

A Tor Book
Published by Tom Doherty Associates, LLC
175 Fifth Avenue
New York, NY 10010

Tor® is a registered trademark of Tom Doherty Associates, LLC

ISBN: 0-812-52364-4

First edition: August 1999

Printed in the United States of America

0 9 8 7 6 5 4 3 2 1

CONTENTS

▼

FOR CENTURIES, STORYTELLERS of every land have been weaving imaginative tales of the mysteries and wonders of the universe. The first stories were simply myths of gods and goddesses. The myths were used to explain what were then frightening things, such as a trail of fire in the sky caused by a falling meteoroid, or the darkening of the Sun during an eclipse. Today, science fiction writers entertain us with stories of space travel and strange alien worlds.

Now, with the benefit of spacecraft with such names as Galileo, Pioneer, Mariner, Voyager, and Magellan, and with powerful instruments that can probe far out into deep space, astronomers are learning what really exists beyond our small planet. Many of the things they discover are stranger and more exciting than any fiction. Can you imagine a star big enough to hold 160 Suns, or everything in the universe fitting into a particle smaller than a grain of sand? Have you ever heard of an object that is thinner than a human hair, but so massive that an inch of it would weigh as much as Earth's tallest mountain, or an explosion so powerful that it releases as much energy as would be released by a 100 trillion-trillion-trillion-megaton (91 trillion-trillion-trillion metric megaton) H-bomb? Imagine an object with gravity so strong that nothing can escape from it—not even light; or a mysterious object with an attractive force so incredibly powerful that our entire Galaxy and many of its neighbors are being drawn toward the object at speeds of up to 700 mps (1130 kmps)!

No, these things are not from the pages of science fiction tales. They are a few of the strange and marvelous discoveries that have been made since people have begun to probe the mysteries of the universe. So turn the page and prepare for a remarkable journey as you explore the marvels of outer space.

WHO WERE THE EARLY ASTRONOMERS?

Galileo

ASTRONOMERS ARE PEOPLE who study the Sun, Moon, stars, planets, comets, and other things in space. It is impossible to say when people first became curious about space, but astronomers from all over the world—from China, the Middle East, Africa, and the Americas—have recorded the cycles and apparent movement of the Sun, Moon, and stars for thousands of years.

Astronomy is the study of space and the objects in it. The birth of astronomy in the West began in Greece more than 2000 years ago. Some Greeks observed the sky and searched for answers to the mysteries they saw there, rather than accepting stories and myths told by others. Eudoxus (yoo-DOK-sus), who lived around 400 to 350 B.C., was one of the first Greek astronomers. His explanation for the motion of bodies in space was that they were fixed to huge crystal spheres that rotated around the Earth.

THE FIRST LOOK ▲

ALTHOUGH HE DIDN'T invent it, the Italian astronomer Galileo Galilei built the first practical telescope in 1609. He then became the first astronomer to use a telescope to observe bodies in space. Galileo carefully recorded his observations and became convinced that Copernicus was right about a sun-centered Solar System.

▲ WHAT'S IN A NAME?

FOR MORE THAN 2000 years, stargazers have drawn pictures based on the patterns formed by groups of stars. To them, the star patterns resembled people, animals, and objects. These pictures were something like "connect the dots" designs. Today we call these groups *constellations*, from the Latin term meaning "together stars."

A SUN-CENTERED ◀ SYSTEM

IN THE EARLY 1500s, a Polish astronomer named Copernicus (koh-PER-nih-kus) rediscovered Aristarchus's theories and decided that they provided an interesting explanation of his own observations. Today, most of the credit for the idea that the Earth rotates and the Sun is the center of the Solar System goes to Copernicus. At the urging of his friends, Copernicus explained his ideas in a book called *On the Revolutions of the Celestial Spheres*. The book was not published until 1543, and Copernicus first saw a copy only a few hours before he died.

Nicolaus Copernicus

Sometime around 230 B.C., a Greek mathematician named Aristarchus (air-uh-STAR-kus) suggested that Earth was one of several wandering bodies (planets) that actually moved around the Sun. He also suggested that the stars only *appeared* to move around Earth because the Earth was rotating, or turning like a top. Aristarchus's ideas were considered ridiculous by many of the other Greeks.

Around A.D. 140, Ptolemy (TOL-uh-mee), a scientist from Alexandria, suggested that a motionless Earth was at the center of the entire universe and that everything else in the sky moved around it. He recorded his idea, and a complicated explanation of how such a system operated, in a book called the *Almagest*. Although Ptolemy's idea was incorrect, it was accepted for almost 1400 years.

MORE PROOF

ABOUT FOUR CENTURIES ago, a Danish astronomer named Tycho Brahe took on a young German assistant named Johannes Kepler. After Brahe's death, Kepler used Brahe's observations to determine that each planet moved around the Sun at different speeds. He also figured out that the planets moved around the Sun in flattened oval patterns, or ellipses, not in circles.

Ptolemy

WHAT WAS THE BIG BANG?

MANY SCIENTISTS believe the Big Bang was a great, violent explosion at the beginning of time that gave birth to the universe as we know it. According to the Big Bang

the cosmic egg

theory, our entire universe began with everything that has ever existed squashed into a space smaller than the tiniest grain of sand. This incredibly small unit is sometimes called the cosmic egg. The cosmic egg was also extremely dense, or tightly packed with what would eventually become all the matter of the universe. If the density of water is 1, the density of the cosmic egg would have been 1 quadrillion (that's 1,000,000,000,000,000)! The cosmic egg would also have been incredibly hot, hotter than anything that has existed since.

IT'S A FACT!

MASS IS THE amount of matter that makes up a substance or object. The modern universe is about 76 percent hydrogen and 23 percent helium. This means that these two gases, which were the first to form after the Big Bang, still make up more than 99 percent of the universe!

76% hydrogen

23% helium

the universe

If the Big Bang did indeed occur, it took place about 15 billion years ago. As a result of the explosion, the universal "soup" (which was not yet separated into matter and energy) spewed forth. Within seconds, particles formed as the density and temperature of the "soup" dropped.

P'an Ku

WHAT WAS ONCE BELIEVED

MANY ANCIENT CULTURES developed myths to explain the creation of the universe. The Egyptians of 4000 years ago believed that the universe began as a great ocean called Nun. The Chinese believed that the god P'an Ku carved the universe from chaos. He was said to have used a hammer and chisel to fashion the planets from chunks of rock floating in space. According to legend, the chore took 18,000 years!

Over several hundred thousand years, these particles began to collide. Gases such as hydrogen and helium formed and grouped together in great rotating spheres called the protogalactic clouds. As gravity pulled on these clouds, they eventually collapsed into large clumps. The clouds became the birthplaces of the first stars. Some of the stars burned brightly, but within a few million years, they were ripped apart by huge explosions. The materials that had been formed within these stars then contributed to the birth of a new generation of stars. From the formation of the first stars to the formation of our Solar System, it took at least 7½ billion years.

OLD TIMERS ▶

WE CAN STILL see the remains of early birthplaces of stars in huge groups of 100,000 or more stars called globular clusters. They are the oldest objects in a galaxy such as our own.

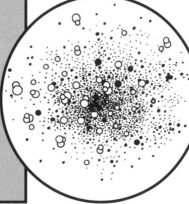

HOW WAS THE SOLAR SYSTEM BORN?

THE SOLAR SYSTEM consists of the Sun and all the planets, moons, and other objects that revolve around it. The Sun and its planets began to form from a cloud of hydrogen, helium, and space dust about 5 billion years ago. Some sort of force, most likely a shock wave from a huge exploding star, caused the cloud to collapse. Soon after, it began to rotate, getting faster and faster. Eventually, the cloud turned into a gigantic spinning disk. The disk was about 50 billion mi. (81 billion km.) across, and it had a huge bulge at the center. Over about 10 million years (or perhaps as little as a million years), the core grew hotter and hotter and began to glow. The temperatures and pressures at the core eventually became so incredibly high that a nuclear reaction called fusion took place, and the Sun began to shine. The birth of the young Sun was violent. It spewed out billions upon billions of particles in a powerful stream known

IT'S A FACT!

LESS THAN ONE percent of the matter that makes up the Solar System is taken up by the planets and their satellites (a satellite is an object in orbit around another object, such as a moon around a planet). Most of the matter is in the Sun itself.

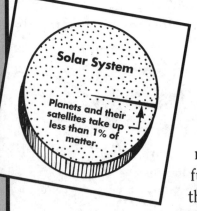

Solar System

Planets and their satellites take up less than 1% of matter.

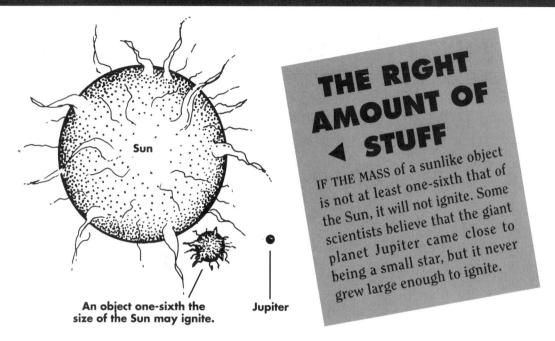

Sun

An object one-sixth the
size of the Sun may ignite.

Jupiter

THE RIGHT AMOUNT OF ◀ STUFF

IF THE MASS of a sunlike object is not at least one-sixth that of the Sun, it will not ignite. Some scientists believe that the giant planet Jupiter came close to being a small star, but it never grew large enough to ignite.

as the solar wind. Over millions of years, the rotation of the Sun slowed and the solar wind calmed.

The planets formed around the Sun from leftover materials in the outer regions of the spinning disk. Bit by bit, over a period of perhaps 10,000 years, tiny grains of dust bumped into each other and began clumping together. Small clumps attracted other clumps and became larger and larger until they were several miles across. Over the next few million years, these small bodies, called planetesimals, continued to sweep up everything in their paths, including gases. Eventually, they formed the nine planets of the Solar System.

THAT'S A LOT OF MOONS!

SEVEN OF THE planets that orbit around the Sun have moons. Some have more than others, but altogether the known moons in the Solar System total at least 50.

CONTINUOUS ENERGY

THE SUN IS a whopping 5 billion years old. Since it was formed, it has been converting about 660 million tons (600 million metric tons) of its matter to energy every second. The Sun will continue to do this for the rest of its life. You don't have to worry about the Sun running out of matter, though. Even at the end of its normal life in another 5 billion years, it will have used up only one-thousandth of its original amount of matter.

WHAT IS THE SUN?

THE SUN IS our local star. It is a huge ball of churning, glowing gases, and it is the center of our Solar System. The Sun is a fairly average star, not especially hot, bright, or large, but without it life on Earth could not exist. The Sun gives us the heat and light that allow living things to survive.

The Sun has a diameter of 865,000 mi. (1.4 million km.) and is large enough to hold more than 1 million planets the size of Earth. The very center, or core, of the Sun contains about half of all the Sun's matter. The temperature in the core

prominence
solar flare
sunspot
corona
chromosphere
photosphere
convective zone
radiative zone
core

WHAT THE HECK *ARE* THOSE?

SUNSPOTS WERE FIRST observed by Chinese astronomers as early as 200 B.C. In 1908, American astronomer George Hale discovered that sunspots contain strong magnetic fields.

▲ WARNING!

IT IS VERY dangerous to look directly at the Sun with the naked eye. Viewing the Sun through a telescope or binoculars can result in severe eye damage and even blindness. Don't take chances!

IT'S A FACT!

FUSION IS A nuclear reaction in which hydrogen atoms combine to form helium atoms. When fusion takes place, lots of energy is given off. The Sun contains enough hydrogen to continue the fusion process for at least the next 5 billion years.

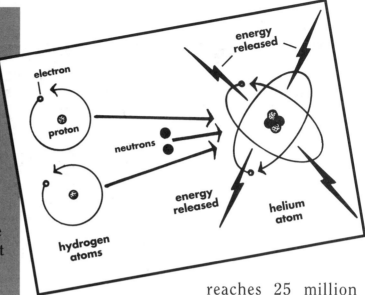

reaches 25 million degrees and the pressure is extremely high. Such high temperature and pressure cause nuclear reactions to take place in the core. These reactions provide the energy that keeps the Sun shining.

Moving outward from the core are the radiative zone and the convective zone. These zones make up most of the Sun. At the surface of the Sun is a region of boiling gases called the photosphere. The photosphere is the part of the Sun that is visible from Earth. It has a temperature of approximately 10,000 degrees, and it is about 300 mi. (483 km.) deep. In fairly regular cycles of about 11 years, dark, cooler areas called sunspots form in the photosphere. Of course, these spots are only considered dark and cool for the Sun. Sunspots are still brighter than the Moon and hotter than a blast furnace.

Above the photosphere is the chromosphere, or "colorsphere." It is a layer of hot gases that reach temperatures of about 50,000 degrees. Stretching far out from the chromosphere is the corona, or "crown." The temperature of the corona rises to an amazing 3 million degrees or more.

THAT'S MAJOR STATIC

▼

A SOLAR FLARE is a huge burst of energy that surges upward from the area of a sunspot. A flare may reach as high a temperature as 36 million degrees and spew out as much energy as a 10-billion-megaton (9-billion-metric-megaton) bomb. In March 1989, the energy given off by a powerful solar flare caused some satellites to drop into lower orbits and also disrupted radio transmissions on Earth.

WHAT IS THE EARLY EARTH?

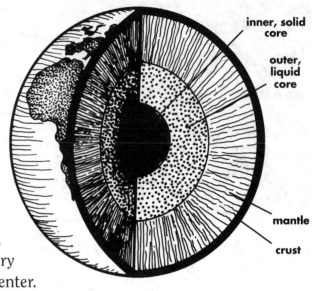

inner, solid core

outer, liquid core

mantle

crust

ABOUT 5 BILLION years ago, the young Earth was just a huge, cold lump of rock and metals, third in orbit around the newborn Sun. But over time, the rock and metals became very tightly packed at the core, or center. This created so much pressure that the temperature in the core began to rise. At the same time, radioactive elements deep within the planet were breaking down and releasing energy in the form of heat. The inner regions of Earth became molten, or melted. Within the molten planet, elements such as iron and nickel sank to the center and formed a solid core. Above this, a liquid core developed, and the liquid core was surrounded by a churning layer of molten rock, called the mantle. By the time a billion years had passed, Earth's thin, cracked surface, called the crust, was bulging with volcanoes that gushed out rivers of fiery, molten rock called lava.

A SPECIAL SHIELD

ultraviolet rays

oxygen released

ozone shield

THE EARLIEST FORMS of life could live only in the oceans. One reason for this was that the water protected these life-forms from dangerous radiation from the Sun. As the oxygen given off by living things built up in the atmosphere, it interacted with ultraviolet rays from the Sun, and a layer of the gas ozone developed about 15 mi. (24 km.) above Earth's surface. The ozone absorbed the Sun's dangerous radiation and made it safe for living things to venture out onto dry land.

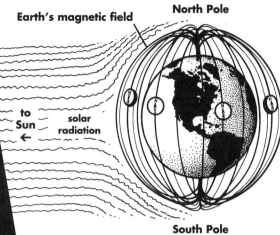

Earth's magnetic field

North Pole

to Sun

solar radiation

South Pole

HOW DID ▶ THAT HAPPEN?

EARTH ACTS LIKE a giant bar magnet, and like a magnet, it is surrounded by a magnetic field. This magnetic field is necessary for life to exist on Earth because it deflects dangerous radiation streaming toward the Earth from the Sun. The field is caused by electrical currents within the Earth, and it can be detected with a compass. How it has come to exist, however, is still a mystery.

Eventually, the Earth began to cool and the surface hardened, forming a solid rock crust. Gases released both from the lava and from molten rock below the crust collected above Earth and formed an atmosphere. Some of the gas bubbling out was steaming water vapor. As this water vapor rose into the atmosphere, it cooled, condensed, and then fell as rain. For centuries, Earth was blanketed by thick, dark clouds, and rain fell continuously. As lightning crackled above, the water rushed over rocks, wearing away minerals and carrying them toward the oceans that were rapidly filling the lowlands. Eventually, the Sun shone. The Earth was on its way to becoming the most extraordinary planet in the Solar System—the only planet we know of that supports life.

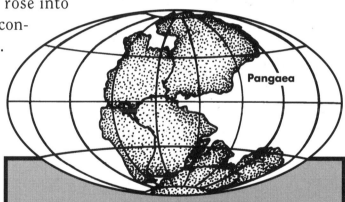

Pangaea

THE CONTINENTS ARE BORN

AT THE BEGINNING of the dinosaur age, around 250 million years ago, there was only one giant continent called Pangaea (pan-JEE-uh). About 135 million years ago, Pangaea broke into two. The mega-continents eventually broke up into the continents we know today.

WHAT IS THE MOON?

Mare Ibrium

Copernicus

Sea of Tranquility (Mare Tranquillitatis)

THE MOON IS Earth's only satellite, and it is our closest neighbor in space. It orbits Earth about every 27 days. It is smaller than Earth, and it has no air, no water, and no life-forms living on it.

On July 20, 1969, the United States Apollo 11 mission made the first successful manned Moon landing. During that mission and those that followed until 1972, astronauts gathered 841 lb.(382 kg.) of Moon rocks for study. Scientists learned a great deal about the Moon, but one mystery in particular still remains. Where did the Moon come from? There are several theories about how the Moon was formed. One theory suggests that it was once a small, planet-like object wandering through the Solar System. Earth then "captured" this object, and the Moon began orbiting the Earth. That

A SPECIAL SEA

THE SEA OF TRANQUILITY has two special claims to fame. It was among the first maria to form on the Moon. Four billion years later, it was the site at which astronauts first landed on the Moon.

FAMILIAR FACE

FROM EARTH, WE always see the same side of the Moon. This is because the Moon spins on its axis and completes one rotation in 27.3 days, or almost one month. It also takes 27.3 days for the Moon to orbit Earth. These two movements work together to keep the same side of the Moon always turned toward Earth.

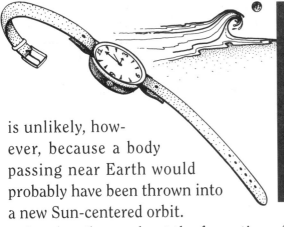

THE TUG OF the Moon's gravity on Earth's ocean tides is slightly slowing the rate at which this planet spins. Today will be about 0.3 billionth of a second longer than yesterday!

is unlikely, however, because a body passing near Earth would probably have been thrown into a new Sun-centered orbit.

Another theory about the formation of the Moon is based on the fact that the Moon and the molten layer of the Earth are made up of many of the same elements. This might mean that Earth and the Moon formed at about the same time and in the same way. But the Earth was larger than the Moon. This made it possible for Earth to tug the smaller Moon into its orbit.

One of the most popular theories about the origin of the Moon suggests that soon after the Earth formed, a huge body almost the size of Mars crashed into the young planet. A tremendous amount of rock and molten material exploded into space. Some of the material splashed into orbit and eventually regrouped to form the Moon. The Moon has glowed in the night sky ever since.

BOMBS AWAY! ▶

AFTER THE MOON formed, it was bombarded by meteoroids, which created huge craters on its surface. There are more than 300,000 of these meteorite craters on the near side of the Moon (the side that faces Earth). Because the Moon has no water or atmosphere to wear away the craters, many of them are in almost the same condition as when they were formed.

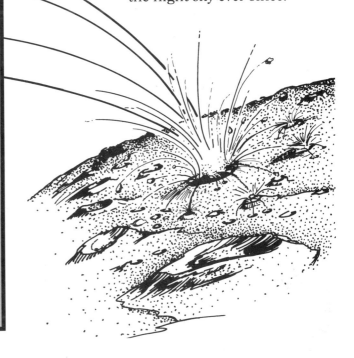

WHO ARE OUR PLANETARY NEIGHBORS?

OUR PLANETARY NEIGHBORS are the eight other known planets in our Solar System. They were formed about 4½ billion years ago in the outer reaches of the cloud of gas and dust that formed the Sun. The word *planet* comes from a Greek word that means "wanderer." At least five, and sometimes six, planets are visible from Earth with the naked eye. You can tell these planets from stars because the planets seem to wander. Over the course of a few days or weeks, the planets change their positions in the sky compared to other objects.

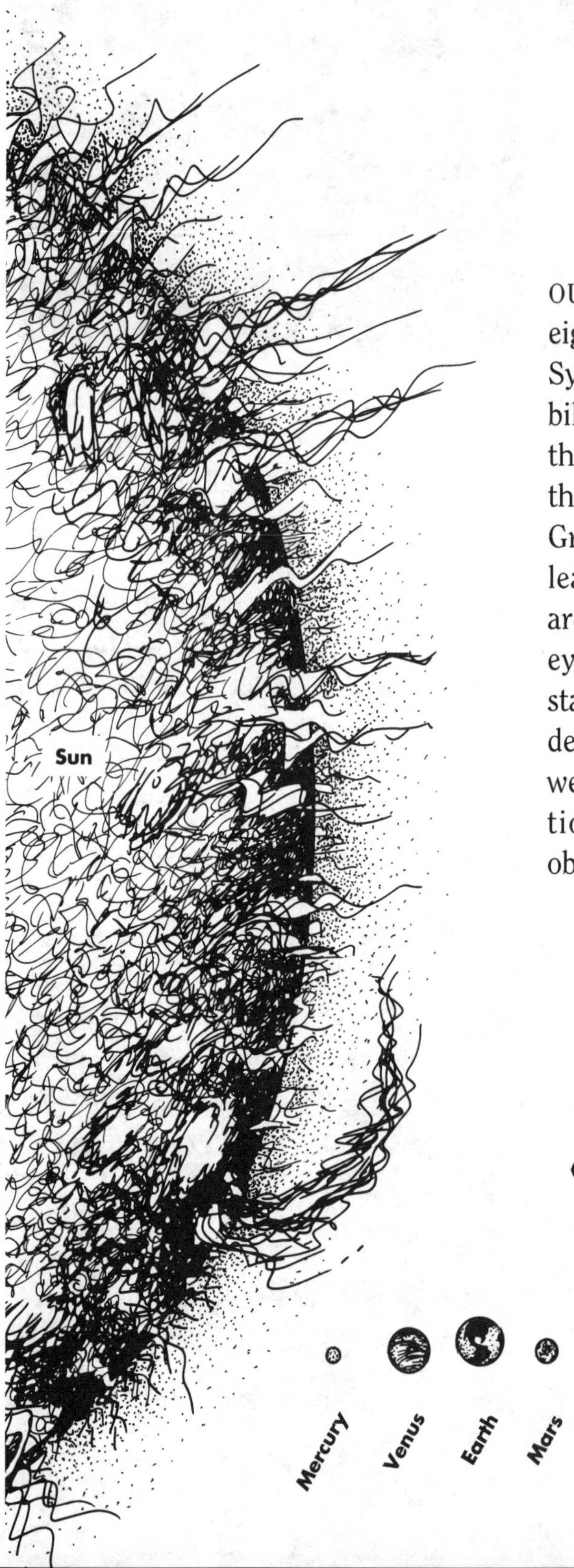

Sun

Mercury

Venus

Earth

Mars

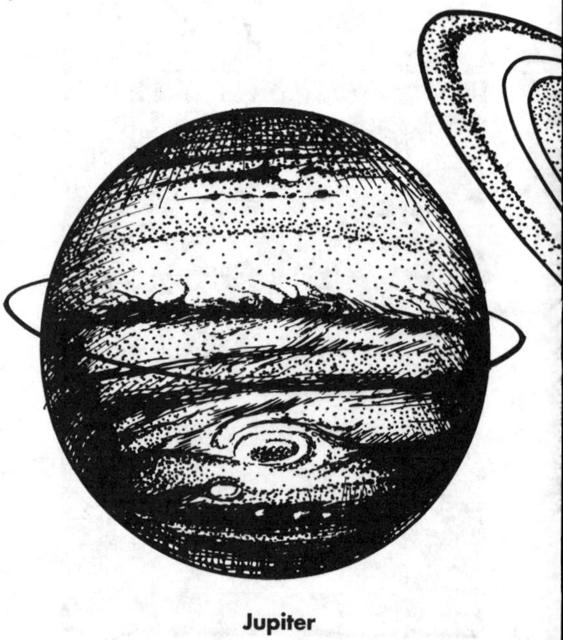

Jupiter

THE INNER PLANETS

Earth is the largest of the four inner planets. Its nearest neighbors are Mercury, Venus, and Mars. Each of these planets has a heavy metallic core and a firm surface of lighter rock. All three are dry, desert planets, and as far as we know, all are lifeless.

Mercury is the closest planet to the Sun. Mercury also has the fastest orbit. It races around the Sun at nearly 30 mps (48 kmps) and completes the trip in about 88 Earth days. Mercury's rotation, however, is slow. It turns on its axis at about 6 mph (10 kmph).

Venus is the closest planet to Earth and also the hottest planet in the Solar System. Temperatures on its surface reach about 900 degrees—enough to melt lead!

Of the four inner planets (including Earth), Mars is farthest from the Sun. Some scientists suggest that simple life-forms may have existed on Mars for a short time soon after the planet formed. The Antarctic environment here on Earth is in many ways similar to conditions on Mars. Some forms of single-cell plants live in parts of Antarctica, mainly in the upper layers of certain rocks and at the bottom of ice-covered lakes. So, perhaps forms of life similar to those in Antarctica may have existed on Mars.

IT'S A FACT! ◆

VOLCANOES ON MARS remained active for millions of years and so grew to incredible size. Olympus Mons, a Martian volcano, is the largest known mountain in the entire Solar System. It rises to a height of about 15 mi. (24 km.). This is three times higher than Mt. Everest, the tallest mountain on Earth. At its base, Olympus Mons is about 400 mi. (644 km.) wide and at its top there is a crater 50 mi. (81 km.) across.

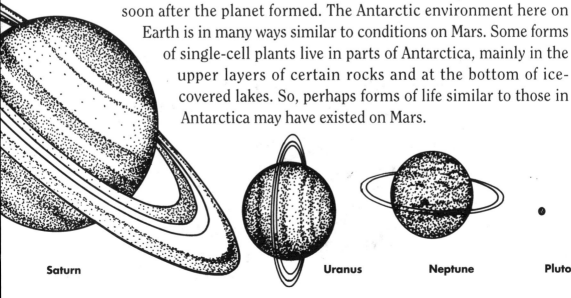

Saturn   Uranus   Neptune   Pluto

← **WHAT WAS ONCE THOUGHT**

THE SURFACE FEATURES of Mars have created an illusion that some people thought was a planet-wide system of artificial canals! The Viking space probes that photographed the surface of Mars proved that there are no canals on Mars. But the space probes did find evidence that flowing water may have existed on Mars. What people thought were canals were actually optical illusions caused by poor telescopes and wishful thinking.

THE OUTER PLANETS

Beyond Mars are Earth's other planetary neighbors—Jupiter, Saturn, Uranus, Neptune, and Pluto. Jupiter, Saturn, Uranus, and Neptune are giant gas planets. These planets have small, solid, rocky cores, but no solid surfaces. Instead, they are surrounded by layers of gases. Pluto is the farthest known planet in the Solar System. It is probably made up of frozen dust and gases, so it is rather like an iceberg in space.

Jupiter is the largest of all the planets in the Solar System. Its mass, or amount of matter, is three times that of all the other planets *combined*. Jupiter is also large enough to contain all the other planets put together.

STORM WATCH

THE GREAT RED SPOT is the most noticeable feature on Jupiter. It is thought to be a huge, colorful superhurricane of gases that has been raging for more than 300 years. The Great Red Spot covers an area as wide as three Earths in a row.

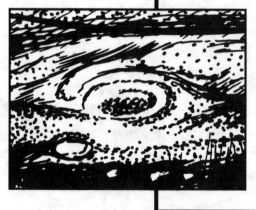

Saturn is the second largest of the planets, and it is surrounded by beautiful, icy rings. Among the very first observations Galileo made in 1610 were the rings of Saturn. With his small telescope, he couldn't make them out clearly, however, and drew them as odd, ear-like bulges on either side of the planet.

◀ IT'S A FACT!

SATURN HAS THE lowest density of all of the planets. Although it is the second largest planet, Saturn is so loosely packed with matter that it would float in water like a beach ball.

A VERY LONG DAY

URANUS TAKES ABOUT 84 Earth years to complete one orbit around the Sun. Because of Uranus's tipped-over position, during its orbit each pole faces the Sun and is in constant sunlight for a period of about 21 years!

REMEMBER THIS!

ONE WAY TO remember the usual order of the planets from the Sun is to use the first letters of the words in this sentence: My very educated mother just sent us nine pizzas.

Because of its tremendous distance from the Sun, Uranus is just barely visible to an observer on Earth. Uranus is unusual among the planets in the Solar System because its axis is tipped over. This means the planet is tilted on its side, along with its entire system of rings and moons!

Neptune is similar in appearance to Uranus, but it is not tilted and it is slightly smaller. A huge storm on the face of Neptune moves westward with the wind at about 670 mph (1200 kmph). At its widest point, this storm, known as the Great Dark Spot, is as wide as Earth.

Pluto is the smallest of all the planets. It has a diameter of about 1500 mi. (2400 km.), or half the distance across the United States. In fact, Pluto is even smaller than Earth's Moon. It is also the farthest planet from the Sun and takes a little less than 250 Earth years to complete one orbit.

WHAT ARE MOONS AND RINGS?

A MOON IS a natural satellite, an object that orbits a planet. A ring is a band of rock and ice particles that surrounds a planet. All the planets except Mercury and Venus have at least one Moon. Only the four gas planets—Jupiter, Saturn, Uranus, and Neptune—have rings.

Compared to the sizes of the planets, most moons are small. Earth and Pluto both have one moon, and Mars has two. The known moons of the gas planets presently total 57. Jupiter has at least 16 moons, Saturn 18, Uranus 15, and Neptune 8. Natural satellites may have various origins. Some may have formed from materials left over after the planets formed. Some may be space objects "captured" by the strong pull of a planet's gravity. Others may be

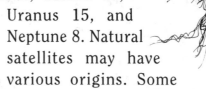

Mercury
Venus
Earth
Mars
Jupiter
Saturn
Uranus
Neptune
Pluto

VOLCANOES IN SPACE

ONE OF JUPITER'S moons, Io, is the only moon in the Solar System where active volcanoes have actually been observed. Io has at least 8 active volcanoes that throw out enough volcanic material to completely cover the surface of Io every million years.

IT'S A FACT!

NEPTUNE'S MOON TRITON and Saturn's moon Titan are the only moons in the Solar System known to have atmospheres.

the remains of collisions between larger satellites in space.

The four giant gas planets are accompanied by more than just moons. Each planet is also circled by a ring or system of rings. The rings of Saturn are the most magnificent. Some scientists suggest that rings last only about 100 million years. That means that if an early dinosaur had looked up at Saturn, the planet may not yet have been surrounded by its rings.

How rings form is still a mystery. It is possible that rings are the remains of moons or other space objects that

wandered too close to the planets and were torn apart by the strong pull of their gravities. Another idea is that rings are partly made up of material from the original cloud of gas and space dust from which the planets formed.

JEWEL OF THE SOLAR SYSTEM

THE BRIGHT PARTICLES in Saturn's rings are icy chunks that range in size from tiny specks to boulders the size of a truck. The rings have a total diameter of about 200,000 mi. (322,000 km.) and are made up of thousands of tiny, thin ringlets in orbit around Saturn's equator. Because of their icy nature, Saturn's rings are the brightest in the Solar System.

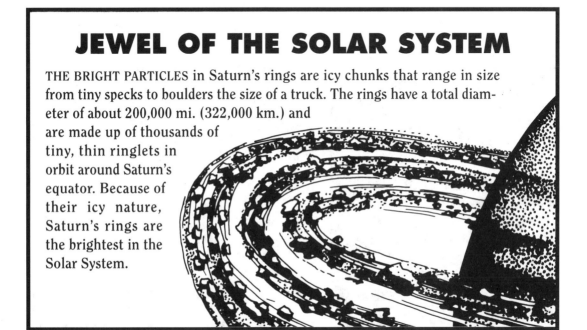

WHAT ARE COMETS?

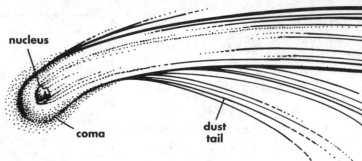

nucleus

coma

dust tail

OFTEN DESCRIBED AS "dirty snowballs," comets are frozen chunks of dust and gas probably left over from the formation of the Solar System. The icy nucleus, or center, of an average comet is from ½ to 10 mi. (.8 to 16 km.) wide.

Many astronomers believe that far beyond the planets, the Solar System is surrounded by a giant swarm of frozen comet nuclei called the Oort Cloud. Within the Oort Cloud, trillions of tiny comet nuclei are drifting slowly in a deep freeze at about -452 degrees.

Occasionally, something may disturb the Oort Cloud (such as a passing star), causing one of the comet nuclei to fall toward the Sun. By the time the comet nucleus reaches the planet Saturn, it begins to change. It gets warmer and releases a cloud of gases and dust that glow around it like a giant halo up to 60,000 mi. (97,000 km.) wide. This halo, which is called the coma, plus the

MONSTER COMET

CHIRON (KY-ron), WHICH IS 150 mi. (241 km.) wide, is one of the largest comets known. It circles the Sun between the orbits of Saturn and Uranus. It was named after the mythological character Chiron, a centaur (a creature who is half man, half horse). Chiron was the son of Saturn and the grandson of Uranus.

THE LONG AND SHORT OF IT

COMETS ARE CALLED either short-period comets or long-period comets, depending on how long it takes them to complete a single orbit around the Sun. Short-period comets complete one orbit in under 200 years. About 150 short-period comets are currently known. Long-period comets may take *millions* of years to complete a single orbit!

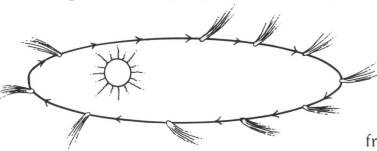

gas
tail

nucleus, make up the head of the comet. Some of the gases and dust may also form a slender tail that may stretch for millions of miles behind the comet. Some comets actually have two obvious tails— the longer tail made up of gases, and a shorter, curved tail made up of dust.

A comet moves at incredible speed in an oval orbit around the Sun. Because of the solar wind, a comet's tail always points away from the Sun. As a comet races toward the center of the

A comet's tail always points away from the Sun.

Solar System, its tail appears to stretch out behind its head. As the comet moves away from the Sun, its tail appears to be in front of its head.

Edmund Halley

RETURN ENGAGEMENT

THE MOST FAMOUS of the short-period comets visible from Earth is Halley's Comet, which returns about every 76 years. It was named after Edmund Halley, an English astronomer. In 1910, Earth passed harmlessly through the tail of Halley's Comet. The comet was last visible in 1986 and is scheduled to return in 2062.

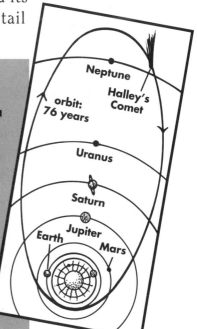

Neptune

Halley's Comet

orbit:
76 years

Uranus

Saturn

Earth Jupiter

Mars

WHAT ARE METEOROIDS?

A METEOROID IS a chunk of rock or metal traveling through space. Sometimes meteoroids travel into the Earth's atmosphere. Racing at a speed of at least 25 mi. *per second* (40 kmps), the meteoroid is heated by friction. This friction makes the meteoroid so hot it burns up, creating a fiery streak called a meteor. Although meteors are often called "shooting stars," these bright trails of light that sometimes flash through the night sky have nothing to do with the stars.

Some meteoroids are actually particles given off by a passing comet as it races toward the Sun. These meteoroids may flash through the atmosphere by the hundreds every time the Earth crosses the comet's path. The result is known as a meteor shower. Many meteor showers occur at the same time each year. It is easy to predict when they will occur because astronomers have figured out when our planet crosses the comets' paths.

meteor shower

comet

IT'S A FACT!

THE TINIEST METEORS are like grains of dust. Every day, about 10 to 25 tons (9 to 23 metric tons) of this space dust tumbles into Earth's atmosphere.

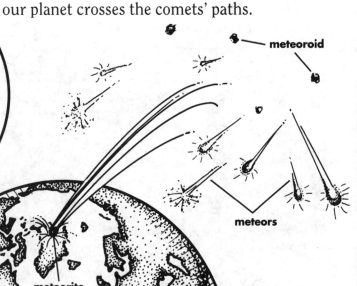

meteoroid

meteors

meteorite

If a meteoroid survives the trip through Earth's atmosphere and lands on the ground, it is called a meteorite. Most meteorites are very small, but occasionally very large meteorites hit the Earth. The largest known meteorite to hit Earth and remain in one piece was found in 1920 in Namibia, Africa. It landed there in prehistoric times and weighs about 66 tons (60 metric tons)! Another large iron meteorite weighing 34 tons (31 metric tons) landed in Greenland. For years, the native people chipped off material from the meteorite to make their knives and other tools!

harpoon head

Barringer Crater

▲ A POWERFUL BLAST

SOME LARGE METEORITES hit the Earth with such force that they completely disintegrate on impact, leaving behind only a huge hole, or crater. About 22,000 years ago, a gigantic meteorite that may have been as much as 150 ft. (46 m.) wide and weighing more than 300,000 tons (270,000 metric tons) blasted out the Barringer Crater in the Arizona desert. The crater it left behind is 4150 ft. (1 km.) wide and 570 ft. (174 m.) deep!

METEOR WATCHING

TO AN OBSERVER on Earth, a meteor shower seems to streak outward from one central area called the radiant point. A meteor shower is named for the constellation in which the radiant point appears to be. There are several major meteor showers every year. This chart tells you when and where to watch for a few of them.

NAME OF SHOWER	BEST TIME TO SEE IT	CONSTELLATION	NUMBER OF METEORS PER HOUR	SOURCE
Quadrantids	Jan. 4	Draco	40+	not known
Eta Aquarids	May 4	Aquarius	20	Halley's Comet
Perseids	Aug. 12	Perseus	50	Swift-Tuttle Comet
Orionids	Oct. 20	Orion	20	Halley's Comet
Leonids	Nov. 16	Leo	10	Temple-Tuttle Comet
Geminids	Dec. 13	Gemini	50	Asteroid 2100 Phaethon

WHAT ARE ASTEROIDS?

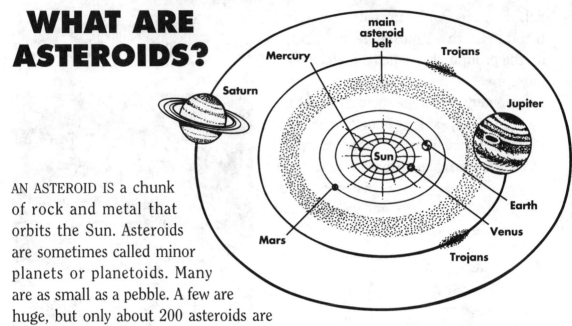

AN ASTEROID IS a chunk of rock and metal that orbits the Sun. Asteroids are sometimes called minor planets or planetoids. Many are as small as a pebble. A few are huge, but only about 200 asteroids are known to be greater than 60 mi. (97 km.) in diameter. Although astronomers have identified about 5000 individual asteroids, there may be hundreds of thousands of them in orbit. Most asteroids orbit the Sun in a 150-million-mile-wide (that's 241 million km.) region between the orbits of Mars and Jupiter. This region is called the main asteroid belt. Two small groups known as the Trojan asteroids share the orbit of Jupiter. One of the Trojan groups races ahead of the planet (these asteroids are also sometimes called the Greeks), while the other trails behind the planet.

Some asteroids have long, stretched-out orbits that bring them fairly close to Earth. These asteroids are called Earth-approachers, or Earth-grazers. At

FIRST AND FOREMOST

CERES WAS THE first asteroid ever discovered in the main asteroid belt. That's not surprising, since it is also the largest known asteroid! This moonlike body was first sighted in 1801, and it measures 635 miles across.

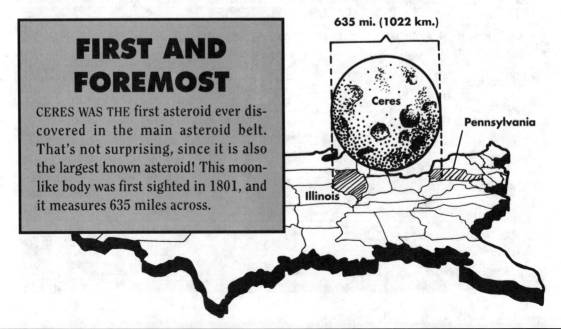

present, about 200 are known. These Earth-grazers are classified by their paths. The Amor asteroids cross the orbit of Mars but do not actually reach Earth's orbit, though they come very close. Ganymed, the largest Amor asteroid, is 25 mi. (40 km.) long. Two known asteroid groups do cross the Earth's orbit—the Aten asteroids and the Apollo asteroids. In 1976, the first Aten asteroid, Ra-Shalom, was sighted. In 1937, Hermes, a small Apollo asteroid, came within 500,000 mi. (801,000 km.) of Earth. On March 23, 1989, there was an even closer call. An asteroid now known as 1989 FC came within 400,000 mi. (644,000 km.) of Earth. It was estimated to be a quarter mile in diameter and to weigh about 50 million tons (45 million metric tons). Amazingly, no one noticed the visitor until several days after it passed by Earth and was speeding away at a rate of 44,000 mph (70,800 kmph).

an asteroid crossing Earth's orbit

Mercury

Apollo asteroids

Sun

Aten asteroids

Venus   Earth

Mars

▶ JUST IN CASE

SEVERAL SCIENTIFIC COMMITTEES have been set up to study methods of stopping an incoming asteroid that might threaten Earth. One plan is to nudge the asteroid out of the way with the explosion of a neutron bomb. The bomb would be carried to its target by a rocket.

WHAT WAS ONCE BELIEVED

AROUND 1802, HEINRICH Olbers, a German astronomer, discovered several asteroids. He suggested that asteroids were the remains of a large planet that had once orbited in the area of the main asteroid belt. Now scientists are certain that no planet ever existed in this region. It is more likely that asteroids are leftover material from the formation of the Solar System.

WHAT WAS THE TUNGUSKA EVENT?

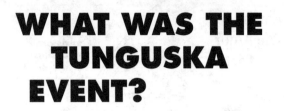

THE TUNGUSKA EVENT was a huge explosion that occurred over the Tunguska River region of central Siberia in Russia. On the morning of June 30, 1908, a bluish-white fireball suddenly blazed in the sky, followed by a blast so powerful that trees were knocked to the ground and burned over an area of 800 sq. mi. (2072 sq. km.). The area of Siberia where the blast took place was extremely remote and difficult to reach. Because of this, almost 20 years passed before scientists visited the scene. In 1927, when scientists arrived to investigate, they were quite surprised at what they found. Actually, they were more surprised by what they *didn't* find. They did not find a crater. The only explanation the scientists could give was that the mysterious fireball exploded in midair—with a blast equal to the force of 30 million tons (27 million metric tons) of dynamite. Since 1927, a few clues have been found that have led some researchers to speculate that the culprit was a small chunk of space rock that disintegrated in the air.

FAR-AWAY FIRE

WITNESSES TO THE Tunguska explosion, from villages as far away as 250 mi. (402 km.), claimed to have seen a huge pillar of fire rise high into the air. The sound was heard as far as 600 mi. (966 km.) away.

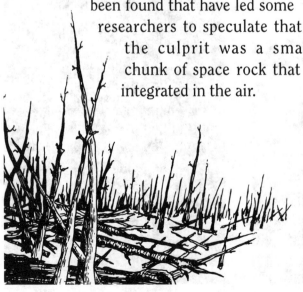

TIMBER ◀ TUMBLER

THE BLAST AT Tunguska knocked down trees covering a half million acres of forest area. The trees looked like matchsticks thrown around on the forest floor.

WHAT WAS THE DINOSAUR DESTROYER?

SOME SCIENTISTS HAVE suggested that the dinosaur destroyer was a huge rock from space that crashed into Earth around 65 million years ago. In 1978, a geologist named Walter Alvarez was investigating rock formations in Italy. Within the rocks, Alvarez discovered a thin layer of clay that appeared to have been deposited about 65 million years ago. The clay contained an unusually large amount of an element called iridium. This element is very rare in the Earth's crust. But it is plentiful in meteorites and asteroids.

These findings led scientists to suggest that the layer of clay was the end result of the crash of an asteroid (or meteorite) about 6 mi. (10 km.) in diameter. The effects of this collision would have been felt around the world. An enormous amount of dust would have been thrown up into the atmosphere, quickly forming a thick cloud that would have cut off warmth and light from the Sun. Without sunlight, plants would have died out. Many animals that fed on the plants, including plant-eating dinosaurs, would also have died of starvation. Finally, many animals that fed on other animals, including meat-eating dinosaurs, would also have died out. So, if this theory is correct, the dinosaur destroyer that ended the reign of the dinosaurs may have come from space.

WHERE'S THE CRATER?

RECENTLY, A CRATER more than 100 mi. (161 km.) wide was detected on the sea bottom at the tip of the Yucatan Peninsula. This crater is considered to be the most likely place where a huge asteroid may have slammed into Earth.

WHAT ARE THE UNKNOWN PLANETS?

THE SOLAR SYSTEM is full of mysteries and surprises. Scientists are always searching the skies to discover unknown objects and to solve their mystery. In the 19th century, astronomers proposed that there might be a planet between Mercury and the Sun. Some astronomers actually thought they had detected such a planet. They named it Vulcan after the ancient Roman god of fire. Although they proved to be incorrect, Vulcan became famous in the 1960s as the fictional home planet of Star Trek's Mr. Spock.

According to some astronomers' calculations, something seems to be disturbing the orbits of Uranus and Neptune.

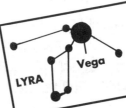

LYRA
Vega

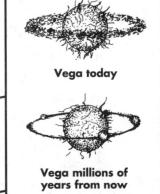

Vega today

Vega millions of years from now

PLANETS BEYOND THE SOLAR SYSTEM

ASTRONOMERS TODAY BELIEVE they have discovered at least two planets circling a dense, spinning star 1300 light-years from the Sun. After noticing a change in the pulsing signal given off by the star, the astronomers figured out that one of the planets is nearly three times Earth's size and the other planet is even slightly larger than that.

↑ IT'S A FACT!

THE BRIGHT STAR Vega in the constellation Lyra appears to have a wide disk of dust around it. Over the next several million years, this dust could form into planets.

WHAT WE ONCE THOUGHT

AT ONE TIME, Planet X was used as a convenient explanation for the positions of some of the objects in the outer Solar System. The theory went something like this: Hundreds of thousands of years ago, Planet X passed very close to Neptune. This caused Neptune's moons to be juggled. Nereid was thrown into an extremely wide orbit, the orbit of Triton was reversed, and Pluto was thrown into orbit as a planet around the Sun. Now astronomers realize that Planet X was not responsible for this arrangement.

Astronomer Clyde Tombaugh was looking for the source of these disturbances when he discovered the planet Pluto in 1930. The tiny planet was too small to explain the disturbances, so astronomers continued to search for what became known as Planet X. New evidence, however, shows that errors in the calculations are probably responsible for what appeared to be the disturbances in the orbits of Uranus and Neptune. Searching for Planet X seems to be just a wild goose chase. Still, there may be other unknown objects traveling in the outer Solar System. Even as you read this page, somewhere on Earth, astronomers are scanning the heavens and continuing the search.

HURRY UP AND WAIT

SOME ASTRONOMERS continue to look for Planet X. But they do not simply search the sky. Their first job is to calculate by computer where the planet's path might carry it. They then turn their instruments in that direction. The tremendous distance from Earth, however, makes objects in the outer reaches of the Solar System extremely difficult to locate with traditional equipment such as telescopes. If there is another large body circling the Sun, robot explorers or space probes may be the best way to find it.

Clyde Tombaugh

WHAT ARE INCREDIBLE DISTANCES?

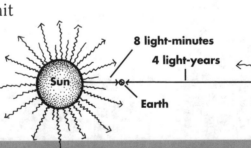

Proxima: 4 light-years

The Sun: 93 million miles

LMC X-3: 170,000 light-years

61 Cygni: 9 light-years

Triangulum Galaxy: 2.3 light-years

Arcturus: 36 light-years

Andromeda: 2 million light-years

THE TEMPERATURES OF objects in the universe are so high, and the distances between them so great, that astronomers do not work with ordinary measures. To make it easier to understand these great distances, astronomers have developed several special measuring units. An astronomical unit, or AU, is roughly the average distance between the Sun and Earth, or about 93 million mi. (150 million km.). It would take a person walking 3 mph (5 kmph) about 3500 years to walk one AU!

A light-year is another unit scientists use to describe great distances in space. It is the distance that light travels through space in one Earth year, or about 6 trillion mi. (10 trillion km.). There are 63,240 AUs in one light-year. It would take a person driving a car at 55 mph (89 kmph) more than 12 million years to travel 1 light-year.

The parsec is a unit used to measure distances beyond our Solar System. One parsec equals about 3¼ light-years, and

8 light-minutes

4 light-years

Sun

Earth

Proxima Centauri

LIGHT FROM THE PAST

WHEN ASTRONOMERS LOOK at faraway stars, they are actually getting information about how the stars looked in the past. For example, it takes 8 minutes for light to travel from the Sun to Earth. The farther away an object is in space, the longer it takes for the light to reach Earth and the older the image is. Light from Proxima Centauri, the nearest star aside from the Sun, left Proxima more than 4 years ago. So, the image we see of Proxima is already more than 4 years old. When astronomers observe an object millions of light-years away, they are seeing light that left the object millions of years before! Some astronomers refer to this light as "fossil light" because they are seeing images from the long-ago past.

1000 parsecs equals one kiloparsec. The Sun is about 8½ kiloparsecs from the center of our Galaxy, which is a collection of billions of stars stretched across space. A megaparsec equals 1 million parsecs. The Sun is a little more than 5 megaparsecs from the edge of the universe as we know it!

A special scale is needed to measure temperatures in space. Temperatures of things here on Earth are often measured using the Fahrenheit scale. On this scale, water freezes at 32 degrees and boils at 212 degrees. Scientists, however, usually use the Celsius scale in which 0 is freezing and 100 degrees is boiling. The scale used to measure very high and very low temperatures in space is called the Kelvin scale. Degrees on this scale are called kelvins. Room temperature on the Kelvin scale is about 300 kelvins. Water freezes at 273 kelvins and boils at 373 kelvins.

BIO BIT

THE GERMAN mathematician Friedrich Bessel was the first person to measure the distance to a star beyond our Sun using the parallax method. In 1838, Bessel found the distance to a star called 61 Cygni to be about 9 light-years. Modern measurements show that 61 Cygni indeed is about 9 light-years away!

Earth's orbit

Earth in January

Sun

Earth in July

parallax angle

apparent path of unknown star as seen against distant star

unknown star

position of unknown star measured against position of distant star

JUST HOW FAR IS IT?

SCIENTISTS USE THE parallax method to measure the distances of many objects in space. They measure the position of an unknown distant star against the position of even more distant stars. They take two measurements at different times in the Earth's orbit around the Sun, say, in January and July. Those measurements give scientists a parallax angle, from which they can determine the distance of the unknown star.

WHAT IS A GALAXY?

A GALAXY IS a grouping of billions of stars, gas, and dust held together by gravity. Galaxies are classified by shape. An elliptical galaxy is round or slightly oval with a smooth and even appearance. A spiral galaxy is a flattened disk with a central bulge and spiral arms. A barred spiral galaxy is fairly smooth with a thin, center bar and a long pair of spiral arms at each end. There are also irregular galaxies that have no definite shape. Tiny dwarf galaxies also exist. A dwarf galaxy has only a few million stars. Our Galaxy, the Milky Way, is a spiral galaxy.

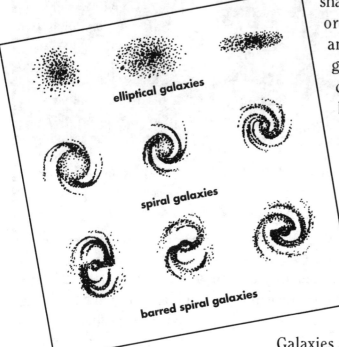

elliptical galaxies

spiral galaxies

barred spiral galaxies

Galaxies are generally found in groups, or clusters. The Milky Way belongs to a small group called the Local Group, which consists of as many as 30 galaxies and covers an area about 5 million light-years across. On a scale in which 1 in. (2.54 cm.) stands for 1 light-year, the distance across the Local Group is about

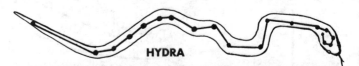

HYDRA

AT THE VERY LEAST

ASTRONOMERS TODAY ACCEPT that at least 100 billion galaxies exist in the universe. They also agree that the number of galaxies could be much higher!

LOOKING AHEAD ⬆

ALTHOUGH SOME FORCE in the direction of the constellation Virgo is tugging at the Milky Way, our Galaxy and other nearby galaxies are actually moving toward the constellation Hydra. Hydra can be seen each spring from the Northern Hemisphere. When you face the southwest, the constellation appears just over the horizon at about midnight.

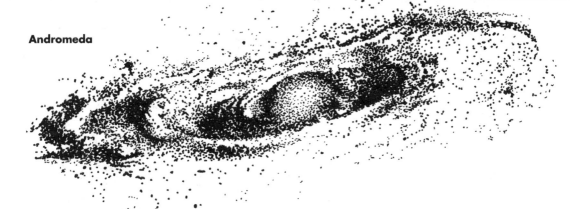

Andromeda

80 miles (129 km.)! The largest galaxies in the Group are our own Milky Way and the Andromeda Galaxy. Together these two galaxies make up 70 percent of the mass in the Local Group. The Andromeda Galaxy is the larger of the two. It is a spiral galaxy whose disk is from 130,000 to 180,000 light-years in diameter.

In 1784, the French astronomer Charles Messier made a catalog of objects other than stars in the night sky. He was actually searching for comets, and the catalog was meant to point out objects that might be mistaken for comets. Messier's list included 103 such objects, and he gave each a number. Some of these objects turned out to be small groups of stars. Others were thick clouds of gas and dust called planetary nebulae. Still others were galaxies. Messier, or M, numbers are still used today to identify these objects. For example, the Andromeda Galaxy is also known as M31.

IT DEPENDS ON WHERE YOU LOOK

TO AN OBSERVER on Earth, galaxies seem to be fairly evenly distributed across the sky except for an "empty" area near the handle of the Big Dipper. In this area, no galaxies are visible. However, with a large telescope, half a million galaxies are visible in the bowl section of the Big Dipper.

LOCAL DWARF

THE FIRST OBJECT proven to be outside our Galaxy was a dwarf galaxy, NGC 6822. It was discovered by Edwin Hubble in the 1920s. Hubble estimated the galaxy to be about 1 million light-years away, but it is actually farther.

Edwin Hubble

WHAT IS THE MILKY WAY?

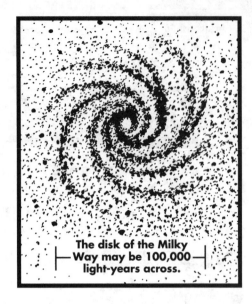

The disk of the Milky Way may be 100,000 light-years across.

THE MILKY WAY is the name of our Galaxy. It is a spiral galaxy containing the Solar System and at least 200 billion stars. This works out to about 40 stars for every person on Earth!

Imagine how hard it would be to figure out what you look like if you never look in a mirror. Scientists trying to figure out the nature of the Milky Way have a similar problem because there is no way they can step out of the Galaxy and take a look at it. Still, scientists have been able to determine that the Milky Way is a spiral galaxy about twice the size and brightness of the average galaxy.

For the most part, the Galaxy is made up of older red stars located in the bulge at the center of the main disk, surrounded by younger stars. The stars in the Galaxy's central bulge are as close as light-weeks apart. Some stars are just light-days apart! A huge black hole—the incredibly dense remains of a collapsed star—may be at the very center of the Milky Way. And swirling out from the center are as many as nine spiral arms.

The Milky Way

SAGITTARIUS

WHAT WAS ONCE BELIEVED

IF YOU LOOK up at the constellation Sagittarius in the night sky you will see what appears to be a band of light. You are looking toward the center of the Milky Way. Several thousand years ago, Chinese stargazers called this bright band *Tien Ho*, which means "celestial river." The Chinese thought the stars in the band of light were tiny fish that swam in the heavenly river. ▶

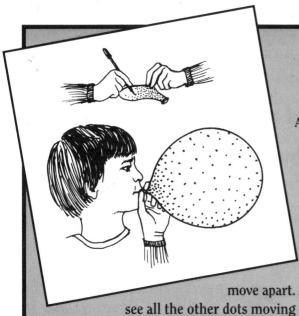

SEE FOR YOURSELF

ALL THE GALAXIES in the universe, including the Milky Way, are moving away from each other. That's because the universe itself is expanding. To see how this works, you need a balloon and a marking pen. Before you blow up the balloon, use the pen to draw fairly evenly spaced dots all over the balloon. When you blow up the balloon, the dots move apart. An observer on any one of the dots would see all the other dots moving away, as if his or her dot were at the center. Actually, none of the dots is at the center. Since the balloon is expanding evenly in all directions, all the dots move with it.

The main disk of the Milky Way is thought to be about 100,000 light-years across but no more than 6000 light-years thick. This makes it look something like a galactic pancake. When the faint halo that surrounds the Galaxy is included, the Milky Way may measure as much as 300,000 light-years across. Beyond the halo, there may be a galactic corona, or superhalo, made up of dark matter that cannot be seen with telescopes. The speed at which the Galaxy rotates seems to indicate that this invisible corona exists. If so, the Milky Way may actually measure from 500,000 to 700,000 light-years across.

IT'S A FACT!

IF THE MILKY WAY were the size of the United States, the Sun would be smaller than a grain of sand on the beach.

WHAT'S IN A NAME?

MANY CENTURIES AGO, people did not know that the misty band of light they saw in the night sky was made up of billions of stars. They thought it was made up of milk, and it came to be known as *galaxias*, which in Greek means "milky way." Since that time, the word *galaxy* has come to mean any collection of billions of stars.

WHAT ARE BINARY STARS?

BINARY STARS, OR double stars, are two stars held close together by gravity. They travel together through space and revolve around a single, common center of gravity. This common center of gravity around which the two stars rotate is called the barycenter. The stars in a binary pair may be quite close or a great distance apart. An example of a very close system would be two stars that are never farther apart than the size of the orbit of Mercury. An example of a very large system would be stars that are so far apart that it takes a few million years to complete a single orbit.

There are several different kinds of binary stars. Visual binaries are two stars that, to the naked eye, appear to be very close together or even one star. Visual binaries can usually be seen as two stars through a telescope. Eclipsing binaries can be detected because the orbit of one star carries it in front of the other star and

orbit of first star

barycenter

orbit of second star

THE STARS NEXT DOOR ▶

THE NEAREST STAR to Earth, after the Sun, is Proxima Centauri in the constellation Centaurus. It is about 4 light-years away. This small red star is too dim to see. In fact, it is one of the dimmest stars known. Proxima Centauri is part of a system that includes Alpha Centauri, which itself is a binary star. Beta Centauri is also very close, but don't let that confuse you. It is not part of the system.

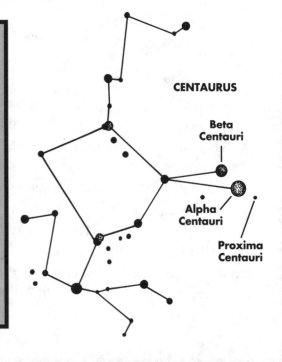

CENTAURUS

Beta Centauri

Alpha Centauri

Proxima Centauri

PERSEUS

Algol

◄ THE EVIL EYE

IN THE CONSTELLATION Perseus, the image of the mythical young warrior Perseus is thought to be holding the cut-off head of Medusa, a horrible monster with snakes for hair. Because the star Algol, which represents the eye of Medusa, is a part of an eclipsing binary system, the eye of Medusa seems to wink every few days. Each wink lasts for about 10 hours!

eclipses it. This makes the partner star appear to "blink." In astrometric binaries, one star is usually too dim to be seen even through a telescope. But astronomers know the partner exists because it causes the visible star to wobble. Spectroscopic binaries are two stars that are so close that they appear as one star. A special instrument called a spectroscope is needed to detect the presence of both stars.

Alcor

Mizar

BIG DIPPER

How do binary stars form? Scientists believe they form when the original cloud of gas and dust that produces a star breaks up before actual star formation begins. The way in which the cloud breaks up results in a wide range of distances between the stars that eventually form. Gravity keeps the stars together after they develop.

NOW BOARDING

IF YOU BOARDED a jet headed for Alpha Centauri, it would take about 5 million years before you would have to buckle your seat belt for landing.

STARRY EYE CHART

AN OPTICAL DOUBLE star is two stars that appear to be close together but are not. The stars Alcor and Mizar are an optical double star in the handle of the Big Dipper. If you look closely, it is easy to make out the two stars. To Arabs living in the 14th century, this pair of stars was known as *Al Sadak*, or "the test." The stars were given this name because they were used as an eye test to check people's vision. Alcor and Mizar are in fact about ¼ light-year apart and are not a binary pair.

WHAT IS A VARIABLE STAR?

A VARIABLE STAR is a star whose brightness changes over time and often at regular intervals of hours, months, or years. Magnitude refers to the apparent brightness of a star to an observer on Earth. A star's magnitude is usually indicated by a number. Zero indicates the brightest stars, although a few stars are so bright that they are given minus numbers. Six indicates the faintest stars that can be seen with the naked eye.

An intrinsic variable star is a star

Some variable stars shrink and swell regularly.

that experiences changes in its diameter or surface temperature. Such changes cause the star to give off varying amounts of light. The most common intrinsic variable stars are the pulsing variables. Pulsing variables alternately swell and shrink. There are three main types of these stars: Miras (named after the star Mira), Cepheids (named after the star Delta Cephei), and semiregulars. Miras are cool red giant stars. It takes 100 to 1000 days for these stars to complete one cycle—that is, to go from dim to bright to dim again. The star Mira, in the constellation Cetus, has the greatest

Mira

CETUS

NOW YOU SEE IT

AN ERUPTIVE VARIABLE star is a star that increases in brightness as the result of exploding. One type of eruptive variable is a nova star. A nova is the sudden appearance of a bright star in the night sky. During a nova eruption, the star may become thousands of times brighter than usual. A nova usually grows to its maximum brightness in a few days. Then it slowly dims over the next month or so.

Henrietta Leavitt

◀ DISCOVERING A "YARDSTICK"

IN 1908, HENRIETTA LEAVITT at Harvard University discovered that certain Cepheid variable stars in the constellation Cepheus brightened and dimmed very regularly. She discovered a link between the length of the star's brightness cycle and its true brightness. A star with a certain brightness always took the same amount of time to complete a brightness cycle. This important information gave scientists a key to reliably figuring out a star's distance from Earth. Now Cepheid variable stars are used as a "yardstick" to judge great distances in space.

range of change in brightness of all the stars of this type. Over a period of about 11 months, Mira's apparent magnitude may vary by as much as 8.

The Cepheids are hot supergiant stars. They vary in brightness on a very regular basis. Most of these stars take from 5 to 8 days to complete one cycle, although some may take as long as 50 days. Delta Cephei, in the constellation Cepheus, has a magnitude that varies from 3.7 to 4.4.

The semiregular variable stars are usually fairly cool giant and supergiant stars. These stars vary in brightness on an irregular basis. Some may suddenly brighten for a while, and others may suddenly dim for a while. The star Rho Persei, in the constellation Perseus, is considered to be a semiregular variable. Rho Persei takes from 4 to 6 years to go from its brightest to its dimmest and back again.

IT'S A FACT!

AT LEAST 30,000 variable stars have been detected in the Milky Way alone.

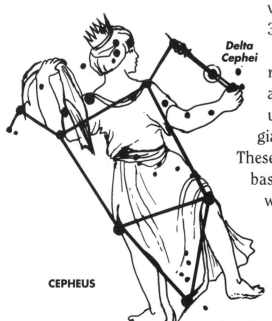

Delta Cephei

CEPHEUS

WHAT ARE RED GIANTS AND WHITE DWARFS?

A RED GIANT is an enormous star that shines with reddish light because it has a relatively low surface temperature. A white dwarf is a very small, hot star in the final stage of its life. Over time, a red giant collapses and becomes a white dwarf. Although average-sized stars live for billions of years, they eventually reach the end of their life spans. As far as galactic events go, the death of an average star, such as the Sun (or a star no more than eight times the mass of the Sun), is calm. After about 10 billion years (in the case of our Sun, that's about 5 billion years from now), the star runs out of hydrogen fuel. Without enough fuel at its core, fusion in a star cannot continue. Gravity causes the star to collapse slightly and grow hotter, then expand into a red giant. When the Sun becomes a red giant, it will be more than 100 times its present size, and it will completely fill Earth's sky when it rises. Mercury and Venus will be swallowed up, and Earth will become a dry, barren, partly molten desert. After a few million years, the red giant Sun will puff away its outer layers and collapse in on

average star

red giant

atmosphere blown off red giant

white dwarf

burnt-out white dwarf (black dwarf)

PISCES

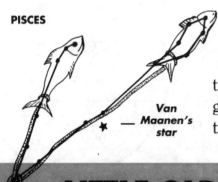

Van Maanen's star

LITTLE OLD STAR

A STAR CALLED Van Maanen's star, in the constellation Pisces, is one of the smallest stars known. It is a little smaller than Earth, but it contains as much matter as the Sun. A 1-in. (2.54-cm.) cube of this white dwarf star would weigh more than 20 tons (18 metric tons), and the pull of its gravity is so strong that a person standing on its surface would weigh 50,000 times what he or she would weigh on Earth.

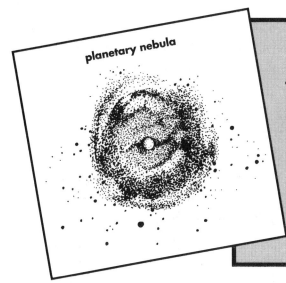

planetary nebula

CLOUD COVER

THE CLOUD OF glowing gas and dust puffed off by a red giant star is called a planetary nebula. The cloud is called this because the first one observed in the 1700s was mistaken for a planet. Planetary nebulae appear in many shapes, including round, oval, ring, and dumbbell. They shine brightly for thousands of years, then they spread out and disappear.

itself. At that point, the Sun will become a white dwarf star, 100 times smaller than its present size. The center of a white dwarf is so dense with matter that a piece the size of a peanut would weigh at least a ton! But a white dwarf has no source of energy, so it is really a dead star. It glows only from the heat produced by the matter in the star being compressed, or squashed, into a small space. Finally, the light from a white dwarf fades out and the star dims into a cold lump of burned-out cinders sometimes called a black dwarf.

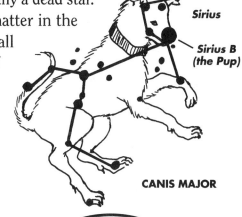

Sirius

Sirius B
(the Pup)

CANIS MAJOR

BIG RED

BETELGEUSE (BEET-UL-JOOSS), THE red-orange star at the shoulder of the constellation Orion, is a red giant. It is big enough to hold 160 Suns, and its diameter measures about 620 million mi. (1 billion km.). Its density, however, is only one one-hundred-millionth that of our Sun. Although it is 520 light-years away, Betelgeuse is one of the brightest stars in the sky and the largest star we can see with the naked eye.

▲ THE PUP

IN 1862, THE first white dwarf star was discovered. It was Sirius B, the companion star to bright, white Sirius. Sirius is also known as the Dog Star, so Sirius B was nicknamed the Pup.

WHAT IS A RED DWARF?

A RED DWARF is a small, cool, dim star that shines with a dull, reddish light because it has a low surface temperature.

Our galactic neighborhood is much more crowded than you might think. Of some 30 known stars within 12 light-years of Earth, 17 are red dwarfs too dim to see. Red dwarf stars are less massive than the Sun, and their surface temperatures are low compared to other stars. In one way, however, red dwarfs are rather spectacular, and that is in their extremely long life spans. These stars shine steadily for as long as 5 trillion years! Because their core temperatures are comparatively cool, they use up their hydrogen fuel very slowly. The life span of a red dwarf star is so long that not a single one has died since the Galaxy formed.

In the early 1900s, the Danish astronomer Ejnar Hertzsprung and the American astronomer Henry Russell each compared the brightness of stars with their surface temperatures. Since surface temperature is directly related to a star's brightness and color, they noticed a definite pattern on their graphs of the stars. On a similar graph we now call the Hertzsprung-Russell (or H-R) diagram,

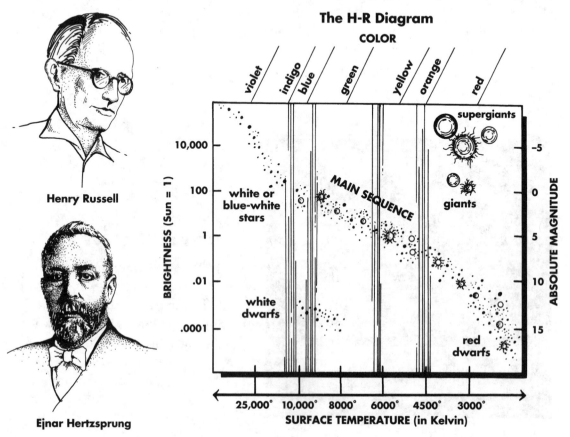

Henry Russell

Ejnar Hertzsprung

The H-R Diagram

COLOR

violet indigo blue green yellow orange red

supergiants

BRIGHTNESS (Sun = 1)

10,000

100

white or blue-white stars

1

.01

white dwarfs

.0001

MAIN SEQUENCE

giants

red dwarfs

ABSOLUTE MAGNITUDE

-5

0

5

10

15

25,000° 10,000° 8000° 6000° 4500° 3000°
SURFACE TEMPERATURE (in Kelvin)

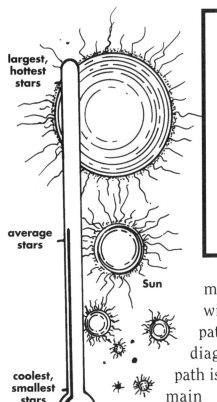

largest, hottest stars

average stars

Sun

coolest, smallest stars

THE AVERAGE STARS

USUALLY THE SUN is described as an average star because it is about halfway between the largest, hottest stars and the smallest, coolest stars on the main sequence of the H-R diagram. However, red dwarfs are likely to be the most common stars in the Galaxy. So, in another sense, red dwarfs may also be called average stars.

most stars fall within a broad path across the diagram. This path is called the main sequence. The stars on the main sequence are those that are still releasing energy at their cores due to hydrogen-helium fusion. These stars vary in mass. Those at the top of the main sequence may have ten times the mass of the Sun or more. Those at

THAT'S FAST!

SOME RED DWARFS are known for their speedy movement through space. Relative to the position of the Sun, these stars may move as fast as 40 mps (64 kmps).

NOT QUITE

SOME STARS DON'T even get to be red dwarfs because they do not have enough mass to make it to the fusion stage. Their surface temperatures are even lower than the surface temperatures of red dwarfs. These almost stars are called brown dwarfs. The dimmest star known is called LHS 2924. It may, in fact, be a brown dwarf.

the bottom may have one-tenth the mass of the Sun. The small, cool, dim stars gathered at the lower right of an H-R diagram are red dwarfs.

Some stars are not on the main sequence. These include the red giants and supergiants (which are cool but also very bright because of their size) and white dwarfs (which are tiny and dim but extremely hot).

WHAT ARE BLUE-WHITE GIANTS AND SUPERGIANTS?

IT'S A FACT!

AT THE PRESENT time, there are about 300,000 blue-white giants in the Milky Way Galaxy. About 10,000 generations of these stars have lived and died since the Galaxy formed.

A BLUE-WHITE GIANT is an extremely large, hot, bright star that shines with a bluish-white light, and supergiants are the largest of the blue-white giants. Blue-white giant stars have the most mass of all the stars in the sky. They may be hundreds of times larger and have hundreds of times more mass than the Sun. Their surface temperatures, too, are many times higher than that of the Sun. These massive stars also have very high core temperatures. As a result, they use up the hydrogen fuel in their cores very quickly. Compared to an average yellow star like the Sun, which lives about 10 billion years, a blue-white giant star has a very short life. It may form in as little as a million years and may quickly burn up its fuel supply in another million years.

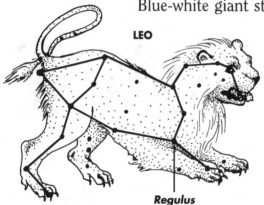

LEO

Regulus

Some of the brightest stars in the night sky are blue-white giants. Regulus, in the constellation Leo, is 5 times larger than the Sun and 160 times brighter. Regulus is 85 light-years from Earth. It has a surface temperature of 13,000 kelvins and a magnitude, or brightness, of 1.35.

The star Spica is the jewel in the constellation Virgo. Spica is 8 times larger than the Sun and it is 2300 times brighter.

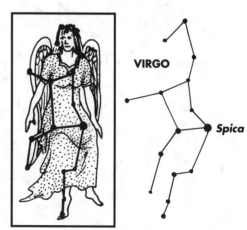

VIRGO

Spica

A CLASS ALL ITS OWN

IN 1859, GERMAN astronomers determined that a special instrument called a spectroscope could be used to study faraway stars. A spectroscope splits up energy from a star into a spread, or spectrum, of color like a rainbow. From this spectrum, the astronomers were able to learn about the elements, temperatures, brightness, and sizes of stars. Several basic types of stars, based mainly on variations in temperatures, were determined. The temperature of each type was also related to the color of the stars. Each type of star was called a spectral class and was assigned a letter of the alphabet. The coolest, dimmest stars were called type M stars. The hottest, brightest stars (the blue-white giants and supergiants) were called type O stars. Today, the main spectral classes of stars are O, B, A, F, G, K, M.

Spica is 260 light-years from Earth, and it has a magnitude of 1.

One of the brightest stars in the night sky is the blue-white giant Rigel, in the left leg of the constellation Orion. Rigel is 50 times larger than the Sun. Though Rigel is 900 light-years distant, it is 57,000 times brighter than the Sun. It has a surface temperature of 12,000 kelvins and a magnitude of 0.14.

IT'S A FACT!

ONLY FIVE PERCENT of all stars are equal to or brighter than the Sun, which is a type G star.

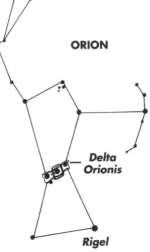

ORION

Delta Orionis

Rigel

SEE FOR YOURSELF

THE STAR DELTA Orionis, also called Mintaka, is a type O star easily located in the constellation of Orion. It is the right-hand star (or upper point) of the three stars in Orion's belt. This star is 20,000 times brighter and 30 times larger than the Sun.

WHAT IS A SUPERNOVA?

A SUPERNOVA IS the explosion of a giant star at the end of its life. Huge stars with eight times the mass of the Sun or more don't die out quietly. When such a star uses up most of the fuel at its core, it collapses under its own weight. Then it explodes in one of the most violent events in the universe, a supernova.

During its life, a giant star converts the hydrogen gas in its core to helium gas. As a result, the core heats up over time, and nuclear reactions produce new, heavier elements such as carbon, neon, and oxygen. About a year before a supernova takes place, the core temperature reaches almost 2 billion degrees. The oxygen in the core starts to turn into the element silicon. Finally, a few days before the explosion, the temperature of the star's core climbs to 3 billion degrees and iron is produced. At this point, fusion cannot continue because to convert iron to even heavier elements would use up energy

The original giant star . . .

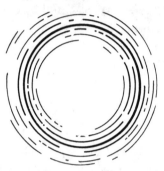

expands to a supergiant.

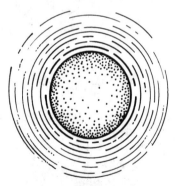

The core then collapses . . .

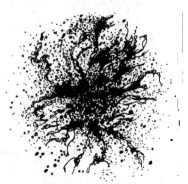

and the star explodes.

IT'S A FACT!

SHOCK WAVES FROM a supernova may have set off the formation of our Solar System.

SPECIAL DELIVERY!

SOME OF THE atoms of the elements in your body probably originated in a distant supernova explosion. Over eons, these atoms may have traveled through space to Earth!

FIREWORKS IN THE SKY ▶

A SUPERNOVA PRODUCES a huge cloud of gas and dust in space called a nebula. Chinese astronomers were the first to record a supernova in the year 1054. The explosion left behind what is now known as the Crab Nebula. The nebula, in the constellation Taurus, is presently at least 4.2 light-years across and is expanding 50 million mi. (81 million km.) *each day*! The Crab Nebula looks like a huge fireworks explosion in the sky. This is appropriate for people in the United States, since the Chinese astronomers first noted it on July 4th!

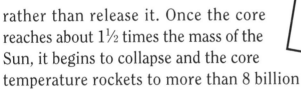

Crab Nebula

TAURUS

rather than release it. Once the core reaches about 1½ times the mass of the Sun, it begins to collapse and the core temperature rockets to more than 8 billion degrees. During the collapse, a core 4000 mi. (6400 km.) in diameter could shrink to just 6 mi. (10 km.) in diameter! The collapse takes place just seconds before the explosion is under way. The core of the star suddenly doubles in size, causing a shock wave to race outward. As the explosion continues, elements such as lead, calcium, and uranium are rapidly formed. The explosion finally erupts beyond the star's outer surface and spews all the star's atmosphere into space. The flash produced by such a supernova is often 100 million times brighter than the Sun. The energy released in a supernova may be as much energy as would be released by a 100-trillion-trillion-trillion-megaton (91-trillion-trillion-trillion-metric megaton) H-bomb!

SPACE CHIMNEYS

ASTRONOMERS HAVE DISCOVERED evidence of remarkable structures in spiral galaxies called galactic chimneys. These chimneys are plumes of gases. The gases are heated to almost 2 million degrees and then shot out into space for hundreds of light-years. Galactic chimneys may actually be the result of tremendous clusters of supernovae.

WHAT ARE NEUTRON STARS AND PULSARS?

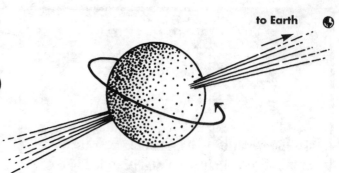

to Earth

A NEUTRON STAR is a small, very dense star made up of neutrons. Neutrons are tiny atomic particles that do not have any electrical charge. A pulsar is a special kind of neutron star. It is a fast-spinning, superdense neutron star that gives off regular pulses of energy.

When a giant star tears itself apart in a supernova, a spinning core star is sometimes left behind. This core is known as a neutron star. It is only about 6 to 12 mi. (10 to 19 km.) across, but it contains nearly 1½ times the mass, or matter, of the Sun. This matter is so tightly packed that a teaspoon of it would weigh billions of tons. In fact, compressing all of that matter into such a tiny area is a little like stuffing the entire state of Hawaii into a coffee cup. The star's gravity is so strong that an average newborn baby on a neutron

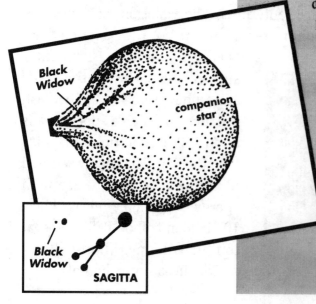

Black Widow

companion star

Black Widow

SAGITTA

A DANGEROUS RELATIONSHIP

ABOUT 3000 LIGHT-YEARS away, in the direction of the constellation Sagitta, a pulsar known as the Black Widow has been discovered. This pulsar has proved to be an eclipsing pulsar. The pulsar's companion is a white dwarf star. A trail of matter from the dwarf star passes between the pulsar and Earth about every 9 hours for a period of about 50 minutes. The pulsar is called the Black Widow because its gravity is drawing in the trail of matter from its companion. The pulsar will eventually destroy its companion, making itself a "widow."

star would weigh an amazing 90,000 million lb. (41 million kg.).

A pulsar is a neutron star that is spinning incredibly fast while releasing charged particles from its north and south poles. A pulsar sprays out beams of these particles in much the same way a lighthouse beam sweeps through space. For astronomers to detect a pulsar, Earth must be in its line of sweep. Every time one of the pulsar's poles is directed toward Earth, we note a pulse of energy.

Today about 500 pulsars are known, but scientists suspect there may be as many as 200,000 pulsars in the Galaxy. Pulsars spin at different speeds. Some are as slow as one pulse every 3 or 4 seconds. However, the average pulsar spins once every $\frac{1}{2}$ to 1 second. About 50 of the known pulsars are called millisecond pulsars. These pulsars complete each spin in a fraction of a second and make as many as 1000 rotations per second. In other words, in less time than it takes you to read this sentence, a millisecond pulsar may have made nearly 2000 rotations!

EXTRA, EXTRA! READ ALL ABOUT IT!

THE DISCOVERY IN the 1960s of pulsars that seemed to be giving off deep-space particle beams caused some newspapers to report evidence of intelligent life outside of our Solar System.

IT'S A FACT!

NEW EVIDENCE SUGGESTS that planets may form around pulsars. Material left over from the original supernova explosion that created a pulsar may form such planets.

WHAT IS A BLACK HOLE?

A BLACK HOLE is the extremely dense remains of a supergiant star. A black hole's gravity is so strong that nothing, not even light, can escape.

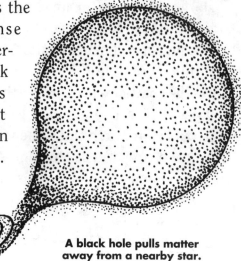

A black hole pulls matter away from a nearby star.

Black holes develop from only the very biggest stars. After a supernova occurs, the core of a supergiant star could contain so much matter that it would continue to collapse. While getting smaller and smaller, the core would get denser and denser. The matter in the core would become so tightly packed, and its gravity would be so great, that it would develop into one of the universe's most unusual objects—a black hole. The border, or boundary, of a black hole's gravity is known as the event horizon, and nothing, not even light, can escape once it is inside the event horizon. The area of the event horizon might be no more than about 20 mi. (32 km.) wide, but the black hole could contain more mass than at least 30 Suns. At the center of a black hole is a point of infinite

A black hole affects only nearby objects.

▲ A HOLE IN SPACE

A BLACK HOLE does not "suck" objects into it from far away. It draws in only those objects that are in its galactic "neighborhood." You can understand this by imagining that a black hole is like a small, heavy ball placed on a suspended sheet of plastic. The heavy ball would sink into the plastic, creating a hole. Any other balls passing nearby would roll into the hole. Now imagine that the ball is so heavy that it creates a hole that is infinitely deep. Anything that happened to roll into the hole would disappear forever. A black hole affects the space surrounding it the way a heavy ball affects the plastic sheet.

AT CENTER STAGE

THERE IS A possible black hole at the center of our Milky Way Galaxy. It is thought to be no larger than the Sun, but its mass may be 3 million times greater than the Sun's mass.

density known as a singularity. At the singularity, matter is crushed out of existence.

Because light cannot escape from a black hole, it is actually invisible. How do scientists study something they cannot see? Scientists can identify a suspected black hole from the way it affects visible stars nearby. Some stars appear to respond to the gravity of a nearby, but invisible, object. As the gravity of the suspected black hole pulls matter away from neighboring stars, the matter is heated to about 1 billion kelvins. In theory, the superheated matter gives off powerful bursts of X rays just before it is drawn over the event horizon of a black hole. Scientists believe these bursts of X rays are evidence of the existence of black holes. In a region of space in the constellation Cygnus, there seems to be a source of such bursts of X rays. This source is called Cygnus X-1, and it is a good candidate for the location of a black hole.

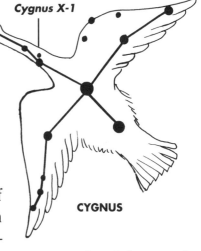

Cygnus X-1

CYGNUS

◀ ALL STRETCHED OUT

IF A PERSON could fall feet first into a black hole, the person would stretch out like taffy. This would happen because the pull of gravity on the person's feet would be so much greater than the pull on the person's head.

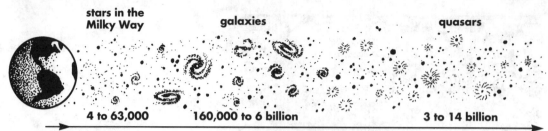

stars in the Milky Way · galaxies · quasars

4 to 63,000 · 160,000 to 6 billion · 3 to 14 billion

(approximate number of light-years from Earth)

WHAT IS A QUASAR?

A QUASAR IS a brilliant object that is more distant than most of the known galaxies. In fact, quasars are the brightest, most distant objects yet discovered in the universe. More than 1500 quasars have been observed, and one has been detected as far away as 14 billion light-years from Earth. Quasars are also the speediest objects known. They move outward from us at about nine-tenths the speed of light.

At first, because they are so incredibly far away, quasars were thought to be huge, dim stars. They are now believed to be incredibly bright galaxylike objects or centers of newly forming galaxies. Quasars are probably much smaller than ordinary galaxies. Most are likely to be no more than 1 light-year across. Others may be no larger than our Solar System, or about 8 light-hours across. But when the radio waves given off by quasars are measured, the quasars turn out to have a tremendous span. The radio image of quasar C345 is at least 78 million light-years across. It is the largest object of its kind in the universe.

radio image of a quasar

Quasars are extremely far away, yet we can detect the energy, such as light and radio waves, that they give off. Some quasars are more active than others. Many are comparatively quiet in terms of radio noise.

WHAT'S IN A NAME?

THE WORD *QUASAR* is short for the term *quasi*-stel*lar* radio source. *Quasi* is Latin for "as if" and quasar means "a starlike source of radio waves."

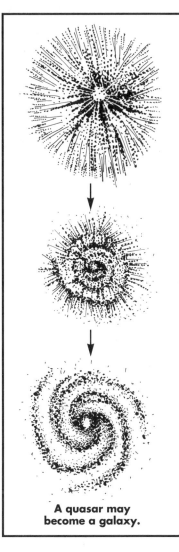

A quasar may become a galaxy.

ONE POSSIBILITY

THERE IS GROWING evidence that quasars are the new-born centers of newly forming galaxies. Because most quasars are so far away, quasars as we see them today formed billions of years ago very early in the life of the universe. Perhaps the quasars we are seeing are actually the first stages in the formation of galaxies. Because we are seeing these quasars as they were billions of years ago, they may have already become galaxies similar to our own.

Others may give off thousands of times more energy (in the form of radio waves, infrared and visible light waves, and high-energy waves such as gamma waves) than a galaxy such as the Milky Way. It is possible that the source of this incredible energy output is matter streaming into a huge black hole at the center of a quasar. At the center of a large quasar there may be a black hole with as much mass as 10 billion Suns put together.

IT'S A FACT!

AN AVERAGE-SIZED QUASAR is about as bright as 300,000 Suns!

THE FIRST QUASAR

QUASAR C273, IDENTIFIED in 1963, was one of the first quasars discovered. It is one of the brightest objects known in the universe. If this quasar was put in place of Alpha Centauri, which is one of the closest stars to the Solar System, it would be about 70 times brighter than the Sun.

Quasar C273 is at least 3 billion light-years from Earth. The light now reaching us left the quasar when the highest forms of life on Earth were single-celled sea creatures!

WHAT ARE SPACE STRINGS AND OTHER THINGS IN THE UNIVERSE?

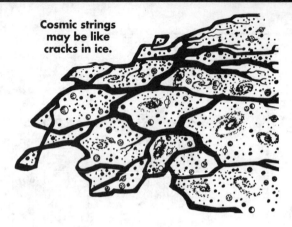

Cosmic strings may be like cracks in ice.

THE MORE SCIENTISTS explore and learn about the universe, the more mysteries they discover. In searching for solutions to these mysteries, scientists predict the existence of some very unusual things. Some of these unusual things are cosmic strings, cosmic wormholes, and a puzzling object or force known as the Great Attractor.

Cosmic strings are thought to be huge flaws, or defects, in the universe. According to the theory, strings formed almost immediately after the Big Bang explosion that gave birth to the universe. As the universe cooled, it began to change from pure energy into energy and matter. This change took place in uneven patches. Defects developed where these patches met, something like the cracks that form when patches of ice join as a pond freezes. Cosmic strings are proposed to be incredibly dense, vibrating loops or lines, thinner than the width of a single proton. No one has yet found positive evidence that cosmic strings really exist.

A cosmic wormhole sounds like something dreamed up by a science fiction writer. A wormhole is said to be a kind of passageway or tunnel in

IT'S A FACT!

ON EARTH, A piece of a cosmic string only 1 in. (2.54 cm.) long would weigh more than the Rocky Mountains!

SHAPES OF STRINGS

IF COSMIC STRINGS really do exist, they could take many shapes, including loops, spirals, and wavy lines. These different shapes may have formed when the strings flopped, wriggled, and collided in space. Eventually, bits and pieces of cosmic strings may have broken away. Loops may have formed when strings doubled back on themselves and broke off.

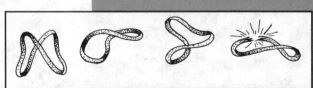

CENTER STRING

SOME SCIENTISTS SUGGEST that galaxies and clusters of galaxies may have formed around cosmic strings. Our Milky Way Galaxy may have formed over time around part of a cosmic string 100 light-years long.

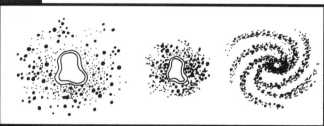

space that connects two areas that are very far apart from each other. Some scientists think that cosmic wormholes may connect two widely separated black holes. Unfortunately, if wormholes do exist, they probably wouldn't work as a means of travel. According to some astronomers, anything entering a cosmic wormhole would be crushed out of existence.

Astronomers have also found interesting evidence to support the idea of a Great Attractor. The Milky Way, and other galaxies within about 200 million light-years of the Milky Way, seem to be racing toward a very powerful attractive force. The galaxies are traveling as fast as 700 mps (1100 kmps). Exactly what is producing this force, however, is still unknown. The estimated mass of the Great Attractor is equal to about 10,000 trillion Suns.

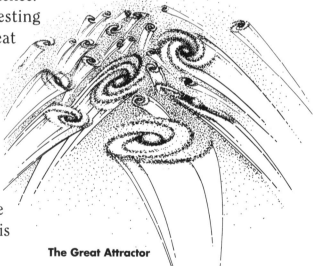

The Great Attractor

COSMIC SHORTCUTS

TO GET AN idea of how a wormhole might connect different areas of space, imagine that you are the size of a pinhead and that space is a huge sheet of paper. To travel from one end of that piece of paper to the other end would take some time. Now imagine that the paper is bent in half so that the edges almost meet, and there is a small hole through both layers of the paper near the double edge. If you simply dropped through the hole, you would travel from one edge of the paper to the opposite edge in no time. A cosmic wormhole might be just such a shortcut in curved space.

WHAT IS THE SEARCH FOR LIFE BEYOND EARTH?

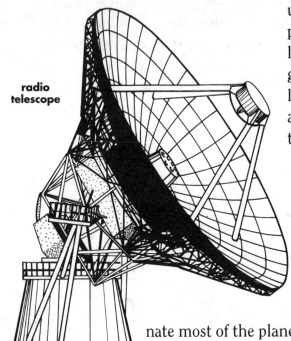

radio telescope

MANY SCIENTISTS TODAY accept the idea that life may exist beyond planet Earth. With the help of radio telescopes and other tools, some of these scientists have been searching the universe for signs of this life. Since there are billions of galaxies in the universe, there is a chance that other planets like Earth revolve around stars like the Sun in one or more of these galaxies. If this is true, there may be life on these planets, perhaps life as advanced as or even more advanced than life on Earth.

Scientists focus their efforts on searching for a planet with the right conditions for life as we know it on Earth. The planet must be warm enough to have liquid water. It must also have an atmosphere that would shield living things from radiation. These conditions eliminate most of the planets and satellites in our Solar System as likely places for life to exist. There is a slight possibility that some form of life exists, or has existed, on Mars, but certainly not in an advanced form.

What are the chances of life beyond our Solar System? A few stars in our Galaxy show a wobble in their orbits that could be caused by planets orbiting them. However, the best chance of finding a planet with life on it is around a star about the

WHAT'S IN A NAME?

THE NAME "FLYING SAUCER" was coined in 1947. An American pilot reported seeing several glowing, disk-shaped objects over the Rocky Mountains. The pilot said the objects were "skipping like saucers across water." Since then, *supposed* spacecraft visiting from other planets have been called flying saucers.

NOW HEAR THIS

IN 1977, TWO Voyager spacecraft were launched to explore space. The spacecraft carry disks that can be played like phonograph records. If an advanced civilization in space were to discover and listen to the disks, they would hear greetings, music, and other information from the people of Earth.

Voyager

same size, temperature, and age as the Sun. Scientists estimate that there are several billion stars like our Sun in our Galaxy. If only one out of every 100 of these stars had a planetary system, and only one out of every 100 of these stars with a planetary system included a planet like Earth, there would still be thousands of possible planets within the Milky Way that could support life. When this is multiplied by the billions of galaxies in the universe, it is easy to see why many scientists believe that we are not alone in the universe.

Frank Drake

IT'S A FACT!

IN 1982, THE International Astronomical Union formed a commission to search for life beyond Earth. The official name for the commission is Bioastronomy: Search for Extraterrestrial Life. It is commonly called the *search* for *extra*terrestrial *i*ntelligence, or SETI.

IS ANYONE ▲ LISTENING?

IN 1960, THE astronomer Frank Drake started the first radio search for life on another planet. The search was called Project Ozma, named after the princess of the land of Oz. The stars targeted were Epsilon Eridani and Tau Ceti, in the area of the constellations of Orion, Eridanus, and Cetus. The search, however, was unsuccessful.

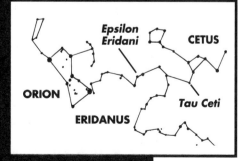

GLOSSARY

ASTRONOMY the study of the universe, including the characteristics and movements of all objects and materials within it.

ATMOSPHERE a layer of gas or gases that surrounds a body in space, such as a star or planet.

AXIS the imaginary line through a star, planet, or moon about which the star, planet, or moon spins, or rotates.

CORE the center or innermost area of a body in space, such as a star or planet. Earth is thought to have a small, solid inner core (made up mostly of iron and nickel), and surrounded by a liquid outer core.

CRATER a large, bowl-shaped feature on the surface of a planet or moon. Craters may form when a meteoroid crashes to the surface of a planet or moon. Craters may also form as a result of a volcanic explosion.

CRUST the solid outer layer of a rocky planet's or moon's surface. Earth's crust is an average 20 mi. (32 km.) thick, but it is thinner under the oceans and much thicker under the continents.

DENSITY the amount of matter, or mass, which is contained in a given space. If two objects are the same size but one is more dense, the denser object will have more mass and will be heavier.

DIAMETER the distance of a straight line through the center of a circle or sphere from one side to the other.

ECLIPSE the covering of one body in space by another body or by the shadow of another body. A *lunar eclipse* takes place when Earth's shadow falls on the Moon as Earth passes between the Moon and the Sun. A *solar eclipse* occurs when the Moon's shadow falls on an area of the Earth as the Moon passes between the Earth and the Sun.

ELLIPSE a curved, flattened, oval shape. The orbits of the planets are ellipses. The orbit of Pluto is the most elliptical of all.

EQUATOR an imaginary line midway between the poles of a body such as a moon, planet, or star, that circles all the way around the body. The equator divides a body into two equal halves, or hemispheres.

EXTRATERRESTRIAL something that originates beyond Earth or its atmosphere.

FLARE a violent, unpredictable release of energy from the surface of a star. A *solar flare* usually occurs near a sunspot or prominence on the surface of our Sun.

FORCE something outside of or apart from an object that can change the state of rest, or movement, or direction of that object. There are four known forces in the universe: gravity, electromagnetism, the strong force, and the weak force. The strong and weak forces are nuclear forces.

FUSION a nuclear reaction in which the nuclei of two lighter atoms combine to make one nucleus of a heavier atom. Tremendous amounts of energy are released in the process. Fusion is the energy source in stars. At the Sun's core, hydrogen atoms are fused to produce helium atoms.

GRAVITY the force that attracts objects in the universe to each other. The force of gravity on an object is measured by the object's weight.

HELIUM the second lightest and most common element in the universe after hydrogen.

HYDROGEN the lightest and most common element in the universe. A hydrogen atom has an atomic number of one, which means it has one atom.

INTERSTELLAR a word that describes the regions of space between the stars. Although it contains clouds of gas and dust, interstellar space is mostly empty.

MAGNITUDE the brightness of a star or other body in space. There are two different types of magnitude. *Absolute magnitude* is the measure of the true brightness of a body, such as a star, calculated as if the star were 10 parsecs from Earth. *Apparent magnitude* is the measure of how bright a star looks to an observer on Earth. Dust clouds in space, as well as the distance of the star from Earth, can affect its apparent magnitude.

MASS the amount of material contained in an object regardless of its size. Two things can be the same size but of unequal mass. For example, a bowling ball and a volleyball are similar in size, but the heavier bowling ball has more mass.

ORBIT the path of an object in space around another body (or sometimes a certain point) in space. Gravity causes objects in space to fall into orbits. The pull of the Sun's gravity, for instance, causes the planets of the Solar System to orbit around the Sun.

REVOLVE to move around another object. For example, the Earth revolves around the Sun, and the Moon revolves around the Earth.

ROTATE to spin around a central point, or axis. For example, Earth rotates on its axis.

SATELLITE a body in space that revolves around another body. A satellite may be artificial, such as a spacecraft, or natural, such as a moon.

SPECTRUM a series of energies that are arranged from long to short according to wavelength. An example is the visible spectrum, which is energy that we see as light. When white sunlight passes through a special glass called a prism, it is broken up into its different colors. The rainbow band of color that we see has a particular order; the color with the longest wavelength (red) is at one end of the spectrum, and the color with the shortest wavelength (violet) is at the other end.

STELLAR a word used to describe something having to do with stars. Stellar astronomy, for instance, is the scientific study of stars.

TERMINATOR the dividing line between the sunlit and dark halves of a planet or moon.

WEIGHT the measure of the pull of gravity of a planet or moon on an object at or relatively near the surface.

ZENITH a point on the celestial sphere directly above an observer.

INDEX